The White House

by Susan Ashley

Reading consultant: Susan Nations, M.Ed., author/literacy coach/consultant

WEEKLY WR READER®
EARLY LEARNING LIBRARY

Please visit our web site at: www.earlyliteracy.cc
For a free color catalog describing Weekly Reader® Early Learning Library's
list of high-quality books, call 1-877-445-5824 (USA) or 1-800-387-3178 (Canada).
Weekly Reader® Early Learning Library's fax: (414) 336-0164.

Library of Congress Cataloging-in-Publication Data

Ashley, Susan.
    The White House / by Susan Ashley.
      p. cm. — (Places in American history)
    Includes bibliographical references and index.
    Contents: 1600 Pennsylvania Avenue — The White House as a home — The White House
as an office — Outside the White House — White House facts — Visiting the White House.
    ISBN 0-8368-4145-X (lib. bdg.)
    ISBN 0-8368-4152-2 (softcover)
    1. White House (Washington, D.C.)—Juvenile literature. 2. Presidents—United States—
Juvenile literature. 3. Washington (D.C.)—Buildings, structures, etc.—Juvenile literature.
[1. White House (Washington, D.C.).] I. Title. II. Series.
F204.W5A84   2004
975.3—dc22   ·   2003062134

This edition first published in 2004 by
Weekly Reader® Early Learning Library
330 West Olive Street, Suite 100
Milwaukee, WI 53212 USA

Editor: JoAnn Early Macken
Art direction, cover and layout design: Tammy Gruenewald
Photo research: Diane Laska-Swanke

Photo credits: Cover, title, Courtesy United States Department of Agriculture photo by Ken
Hammond; p. 4 © EyeWire; p. 5 Kami Koenig/© Weekly Reader Early Learning Library, 2004;
pp. 6, 7, 9, 11 © North Wind Picture Archives; p. 8 © Eric Draper/White House/Getty Images;
p. 10 © Mark Wilson/Getty Images; pp. 12, 15, 19 © Stock Montage, Inc.; pp. 13, 18 Courtesy
Ronald Reagan Library; p. 14 © Dirck Halstead/Getty Images; p. 16 © Mark Wilson/Getty Images;
p. 17 © Richard Ellis/Getty Images; p. 21 © Gibson Stock Photography

Printed in the United States of America

1 2 3 4 5 6 7 8 9 08 07 06 05 04

Table of Contents

The White House is the home of the president of the United States.

1600 Pennsylvania Avenue

Washington, D.C., is the capital of the nation. 1600 Pennsylvania Avenue is an important address in the city. It is the address of the White House. The president of the United States lives and works there.

The White House was built in 1800. George Washington chose the site. He is the only president who did not live there. He died before it was built.

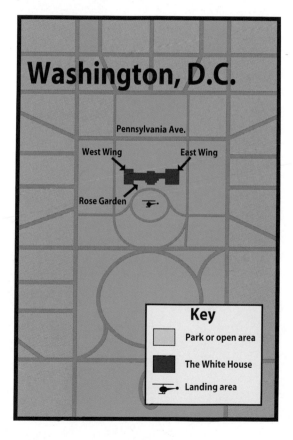

The White House is in Washington, D.C.

In 1877, people arrived at the White House in carriages.

The White House as a Home

John Adams was the first president to live in the White House. The house was not quite finished when he and his wife moved in. There were no indoor bathrooms. Abigail Adams hung laundry in the East Room to dry. Many changes have been made since then.

Many children have lived and played in the White House. Presidents' children have had pillow fights in the hallways. They have roller skated through the formal rooms. One president's daughter slid down the grand staircase on a dinner tray!

President Theodore Roosevelt's children lived in the White House.

The White House has been home to many animals, too. Dogs, cats, rabbits, and birds have lived there. Theodore Roosevelt had more pets than any other president. His son once brought a pony upstairs on the elevator!

President George W. Bush's dog Spot pays a visit to the president's office.

Many of the rooms on the first floor are used for guests. World leaders eat formal dinners in the State Dining Room. After dinner, they often hear music and dance in the East Room. The East Room is the largest room in the White House.

During the Civil War, soldiers camped in the East Room.

Famous baseball player Hank Aaron received
the Presidential Medal of Freedom Award from
President George W. Bush in 2002.

Not all White House guests are world leaders.
Americans who help their country come to the
White House to receive medals. Sometimes
sports teams are invited to the White House.
Many popular music artists have performed there.

Some rooms on the first floor are named for their colors. The Blue Room and the Red Room are used for small gatherings. The White House also has a library, a movie theater, and a bowling alley.

President Grover Cleveland married Frances Folsom in the Blue Room in 1886.

The White House as an Office

President Theodore Roosevelt added the West Wing to the White House in 1902. Today, the West Wing is the busiest part of the White House. The president's office is there. The offices of his staff are there, too.

Theodore Roosevelt made many changes to the White House.

The president and his staff meet in the Cabinet Room. A large table is in the center of the room. The president sits at the middle of the table with his staff around him. Together, they make important decisions in the Cabinet Room.

Ronald Reagan led many cabinet meetings while he was president.

The Oval Office is the private
office of the president.

The president works in the Oval Office. He signs
bills that become laws. He meets with leaders from
other countries. Sometimes he makes speeches
from the Oval Office.

In 1945, President Harry Truman announced the end of World War II from the Oval Office. In 1969, President Richard Nixon called the Moon from the Oval Office! He spoke to the first men to walk on the Moon.

During World War II, Harry Truman spoke to the troops and the nation from the Oval Office.

Presidents Jimmy Carter (left) and George W. Bush (right) spoke in the Rose Garden in July 2001.

Outside the White House

Around the White House are beautiful gardens.
The most famous one is the Rose Garden.
The Rose Garden is close to the Oval Office.
The president often makes speeches there.

The Easter Egg Roll is one of the most popular outdoor events at the White House. On the day after Easter, children come to the White House. They roll colored eggs on the lawn. Children have rolled eggs on the White House lawn since 1878.

Everyone has fun at the Easter Egg Roll.

Sometimes a helicopter lands on the White House lawn. When the president travels, he flies on a special plane called Air Force One. The helicopter carries the president from the White House lawn to Air Force One.

Ronald Reagan's dog Rex greeted the president and his wife when their helicopter landed on the White House lawn.

White House Facts

- The White House has 132 rooms and 35 bathrooms.
- The White House was the largest house in the country until after the Civil War.
- President Calvin Coolidge had a pet raccoon that he walked on a leash.
- President John F. Kennedy's children had a pony named Macaroni.

During World War I, the White House used a flock of sheep to cut the grass.

Visiting the White House

Many Americans have visited the White House. Groups can tour rooms on the first floor. They can visit the East Room and the State Dining Room. They can view the Blue Room, the Red Room, and the Green Room.

Learning about the White House is like looking at a scrapbook of American history. Many important events have taken place at the White House. Each president has left his mark on the nation. The White House is a special place for all Americans.

Many people visit the White House each year.

Glossary

announce — to tell the public

cabinet — a group of people who help the president make decisions

capital — the city where a country's government is located

graze — to feed on grass

laundry — clothes that have been washed

laws — rules that people agree to follow

office — the room or place where someone works

scrapbook — a book with pictures and clippings

site — the place where a building is located

staff — people who work for someone

For More Information

How to contact the White House:

The White House
  1600 Pennsylvania Avenue NW
  Washington, DC 20500
  Please fax children's letters to (202) 456-7705.

Books

Binns, Tristan Boyer. *The White House.* Chicago: Heinemann Library, 2001.

Gray, Susan H. *The White House.* Minneapolis: Compass Point Books, 2002.

Griest, Lisa. *Lost at the White House: A 1909 Easter Story.* Minneapolis: Carolrhoda, 1994.

Web Sites

www.pbs.org/weta/whitehouse/world.htm
www.whitehousekids.gov
www.whitehouse.gov/history/whtour/index.html

Index

About the Author

Susan Ashley has written over eighteen books for children, including two picture books about dogs, *Puppy Love* and *When I'm Happy, I Smile*. She enjoys animals and writing about them. Susan lives in Wisconsin with her husband and two frisky felines.